ITZHAK PE
BROKEN STRING

JACQUELINE JULES

EVENING STREET PRESS
SACRAMENTO, CA

Evening Street Press

April, 2017
Sacramento, CA

Winner, Helen Kay Chapbook Prize 2016

ISBN: 978-1-937347-39-0

Printed in the United States of America

10 9 8 7 6 5 4 3 2 1

For Neal—always in my heart

Table of Contents: Itzhak Perlman's Broken String

Itzhak Perlman's Broken String

Yes, Rabbi, it was a fine story for the
funeral.

It would be nice to believe . . .

I could make music like Perlman
with three strings instead of four,
be lauded for playing my violin
without whining,
refusing to let absence
diminish my performance.

It would be nice to believe . . .
my crippled soul could play
my crippled instrument,
make what is left
produce a pure
and powerful sound.

It would be nice to believe . . .

An urban myth never verified
offers the comfort I need.

Mitzi's Obit

Reading the morning obits
I am stricken to see
Nelly Waldman, dead at age 86
survived by no one.
Husband and son already interred.
No pet poodles, like my Mitzi, mentioned.

Having never met Nelly Waldman,
my grief as I sip black tea
is inexplicable except for the fear
of one day sharing her 3 line departure,
printed on paper soon to be recycled.

From infancy, we are raised
to procreate, to measure our mark
by living blood left on this earth.

It is a sad thing to die childless
unless of course you are Mitzi,
my poodle of 15 years,
spayed in her youth to avoid
the unpleasantness of puppies.

Mitzi's humane end was decided at the vet's
just yesterday. No chemo or surgery
for cancer-ridden dogs. They are privileged
to drift off to sleep with a single injection.

And when I write Mitzi's obit
I will say she was survived
by framed portraits on my mantel—
cuddling on the couch
with a boy too weak to walk.

My Mitzi will always be remembered
as heroic, having been loved by a dying child,
while Nelly Waldman will remain like me,
the pitied mother of a dead one.

A Game Played With Helmets

No one sits down in the stands,
expecting a game
free of fumbles or interceptions.
A perfect game is a fantasy,
even in a third grader's mind.
But when a player hits the ground
to stay, our jaws drop.
Why are we surprised
when little men in red shirts
race onto the field with a stretcher?
This is a game
played with helmets and padding.
If we are going to stay fans,
season after season,
we must accept blood
and broken bones—
times when healing,
for days or even months,
will be required.

Random Headlines

In a zoo in Morocco,
a child leans, smiling,
against a fence, to pose
with the elephant
who inexplicably hurls
a rock at her head.

The next day,
a man in Philadelphia
removes a storm drain
and jumps. Sucked
ten feet into a sewer,
he miraculously survives.

Unlike the child in Morocco.

Reading headlines each morning
I can't decide if the news
defies or declares
a random universe,
one without
predetermined years
allotted each life.

Something to consider
as I stand in a cemetery
talking to a stone
on your birthday,
recall the sound of your voice
in the rustle of a Weeping Cherry
hanging overhead.

The Village Not Reached

The rabbi in the folktale
blessed everything—
even his dead donkey,
before knowing
bad luck saved him
from robbers with knives.

Blessings can hide
in spoiled turnips
and broken wheels.

Who knows if failure
will sweeten later success.

Yet sometimes we must cry
over the village not reached
because the donkey died.

Put down the book
when the candle blows out.

Question the rabbi
surrendering to sleep
on a straw pillow, certain
that everything that happens
must be for the best.

Squatter

Grief slipped in with the crowd carrying casseroles.

For weeks, I didn't truly feel his presence,
being too busy with phone calls and cards.

But Grief was patient,
eating brownies in the basement
until family and friends disappeared.

The day he clumped up the stairs, I was
surprised to see him settle on the couch
in torn jeans and wild hair,
lift dusty shoes on my coffee table,
ask for a bag of chips,
put his palm out for the TV remote.

At first, I treated him as a guest,
hoping he wouldn't stay too long
or eat too much.

But as the months passed and the couch sagged
under his growing weight, it became clear
Grief had no plans to leave.

An unavoidable burden
like sending off death certificates
to banks and insurance companies
kind enough to express condolences
before asking me to sign
yet another form.

Preparing For Disaster

With every approaching storm,
the media drones like a plane overhead,
littering the airwaves with detailed promises
of what one needs to survive.

An obedient citizen,
I store batteries and bottled water
beside neat rows of tuna and soup,
believing myself safe
as long as I have duct tape.

I never questioned the wisdom
of preparing, never linked
the responsible stash of supplies
to picturing
the tallest structures in my horizon
collapsing in rubble
on a warm September day.

Until I sat in a room
with a sink and a scale,
watching a loved one moan
on a cushioned table.

My faith in bottled water has expired.

I can't be comforted by duct tape.

We Want to Know Why

Like the animals in Noah's ark
Everything walks by its mate.
There is no Light without Dark.
No Large without Small.

A front and a back to everything.
Hard, Soft. Hot, Cold. Healthy, Sick.

Still, we want to know why

Up is defined by Down.

Joy sits on a seesaw with Grief.

We are Moses on the mountain
begging to behold a Presence,
allowed only a glimpse
as we cower in the cleft of a rock.

Humbled, we climb down,
stone tablets clutched to our chest,
lay them tenderly in the tabernacle
to carry on weary shoulders,
through years in the wilderness,
always pining for the Divine Face
we won't be permitted to see.

Punctuated Text

Sentences can't go on and on
without a breath.

Pauses are required.

Our lives, like print,
are most clearly understood,
with punctuation.

A simple dot stops the reader,
provides a mental space
between one thought and the next.

Complete or fragment.

The sentence is still over.

Though it doesn't end the questions,
lists followed by a colon, commas
joining words attempting to explain
why punctuation is so cruel.

Why text can't ramble on forever,
meaningless strings of letters,
no one loves, no one mourns.

Letter to 30 Year Old Self

Time recolors every red moment to pale blue.

The colleague who called you "anal"
was correct. The teacher who criticized
your two year old was tactless but on target.

A broken car on the day of a big interview
may not be the worst luck you have.
There are bigger monsters under the bed
and when they reach for your neck
with large bony digits you will regret
past grief over stained white pants
and stolen credit cards.

Patience buys more sleep than pills.

Answers not yet available
should be tucked beneath the pillow
like a baby tooth for the fairy.

Every life is lived on a high wire,
strung over the treetops,
just below the clouds.

Don't expect to feel safe.

Put one slippered foot in front of the other
and balance, arms extended,
for as long as you can.

Train Therapy

Stuck in this dark blue seat,
an oversized purse in my lap,
I consider calling a friend—
someone who hugged me at my wedding
or pushed her stroller beside mine at the park,
one of the many who send e-mails,
saying I'm in thoughts and prayers.

With a cell phone, it's easily done.
Never mind disturbing
all the plugged-in passengers
with half of a weeping conversation
as they type or read on fold-down trays.

Instead, I turn
to the velour-suited woman beside me,
exchange destinations, admire
wallet-sized photos of toothless grandchildren,
wait until she pats my hand and asks about me.

I am grateful she doesn't know my last name,
can offer tissues without needing them herself.
My burdens no more than a sad movie,
she'll forget when she leaves this train,
not luggage a close friend would drag for days.

Ladies Lunch

In between bites,
I compliment the food,
the choice of restaurant
the color of Susan's sweater.

Lila praises my haircut,
Susan nods,
and the conversation circles
an airport the size of Dulles
with news of recipes recently tried,
car repairs, and an organic market on K Street—
never once landing on condolences
expressed three months ago.

They hang in the air
like cleaning products,
a dirty job finished in a room
no longer polite to mention.

I take another bite of salad,
note its salty taste,
excuse myself to vomit,
while Lila asks Susan
if she's noticed, too,
how my face seems thin
since the funeral.

Two Elderly Aunts

With birthdays two days apart,
Evelyn and Eleanor were celebrated together
at the Hunt Valley Inn. Sunday morning
champagne brunch—silver trays of scrambled eggs,
fat French toast, cut fruit, croissants, pastries.

We raised fluted glasses to toast
the triumph of old age, two sisters
nearing the century mark, 95 and 99,
with the same thick white hair,
stylishly cut to frame shrunken features.

A second cousin, invited as an afterthought,
I was seated in the festive party room
across from the eldest aunt, Evelyn,
two grandsons, and widowed daughter-in-law.

Was I the only one to notice?
How my presence beside my spouse
did little to balance Eleanor's larger share
of the table with four married daughters
and ten grandchildren, three with babies
passed from lap to lap.

Was I the only one to wonder?
Why one sister buried a teenage daughter,
young husband, and middle-aged son
while the other remained grief-free
for sixty years of marriage?

The only one to see that Eleanor
was a tiny woman, too frail
to hug all she had, while Evelyn
was taller, with unclouded blue eyes
stretching mottled fingers
across a red tablecloth
to hold hands with what she had left.

Avocado Secret

When the widow wrote
how her husband
once said she was like
a perfectly ripe avocado,
I wanted to rush right out
and buy one. Examine
its tough exterior,
creamy innards,
solid core.

Learn its secret.

At your bedside, I was
best described as a banana.
A fruit turning brown
and mushy too quickly.

Just like an avocado,
when sliced too late.

Except I had no pit
deep inside, stopping
the knife.

Dry Needling

If you stick a needle
in a hyper-irritable spot,
taut muscles will relax,
my therapist says.

I laugh at his silly plan.
Better to tease a tiger
than poke the pain.

My therapist insists.

Find the trigger. Stick
a needle in the spot.
Push till you feel
your grief twist
and twitch.

Disrupt the spasm
pinching the nerve
tighter and tighter.

Re-Watching *Titanic*

Clinging to a raft,
his legs in the water,
Jack makes Rose promise
she will never let go,
she'll die an old woman,
warm in her bed,
not here, not now,
on that bitter cold night,
floating in the North Atlantic.

When Rose keeps her promise
I cover my mouth, shift in my seat,
awed by the girl on the screen.

How did she let go?
Release Jack's body to the dark ocean
let the dead sink and be swallowed.

Why not stay adrift?
Hands clasped with grief.

How did Rose reach for that whistle,
blow and blow through the fog.

How can I let go?

Let the universe
swallow your death
while I reach for a whistle.

Consolation Prize

". . .without the dust the rainbow would not be."
      —Langston Hughes

Raindrops split
white light to reveal
what the human eye
cannot see—

a fleeting glimpse
of iridescence.

Let others skid to a halt,
step from drenched cars,
snap pictures,
quote Langston Hughes.

Not me. I'm incensed
at the sky, how it dares offer
brief spectacle as consolation prize,
after pelting my windshield,
pocking my hood, stealing
the wheel from my hands.

If given the choice,
would I give up all colors
for dull, dependable heavens?

No sudden downpours
no slippery pavement
no one telling me
that windows open when doors close
and rainbows need dust to appear.

Dear Jean-Paul

"Life begins on the other side of despair."
—Jean-Paul Sartre

What makes you think
life needs despair, Jean-Paul?

How many times did you cross that cruel river,
step with damp feet on the other side?

Did you change into dry clothes
trudge forward for miles
only to find another canyon, waiting?

Maybe life begins
when we quiet flailing limbs.
Flip on our backs. Float on our tears.

Maybe life never dawns
after darkness.

Maybe the broken heart
does not beat stronger.

And I exist
on a primal urge
to expel water
from my lungs,
inhale
the next moment
without pain.

The Mystery of Falling Objects

They say an apple
from his mother's garden
hit him on the head.

Created the "Eureka Moment"
when all became clear, a fundamental
law of nature revealed.

Though I find it hard to believe
no one noticed before Isaac Newton
that a glass thrown in anger
sinks to the floor. Somehow
we needed Newton's math to prove
we are vulnerable to falling objects.

At least until Einstein came along
with a theory most can quote
but few profess to comprehend.

Gravity, the reason why
everything on earth is pulled
by unknown forces. Why Prayer
cannot modify what is meant to be.

Yet both Science and Faith insist
nothing is random,
and the universe must be forgiven
when one falling body floats in the air
and another crashes with a deafening thud.

Why Not?

Why not believe?

A soul swirled in a wisp
from your sweat-soaked bed
like a genie
released from a bottle.

Is that more bizarre
than all the months
I trusted in chemo
and radiation?

Stood, head bowed,
prayer book open.

Why not believe a corpse
is just as provisional
as a cocoon?

You will emerge again.

Test bright new wings.

Live somewhere
lush and exotic,
among low-lying clouds,
just like the photo on my desk,
where you stand, bare chested,
arms raised, triumphant.

Two Dirt Roads

The pavement abruptly ended
at two dirt roads
winding off beneath blue skies,
dotted with feathery clouds
in question mark shapes.

Both choices too narrow
with too many ruts and stones.
Yet one had a trace more sunlight
swirling in the dust.

Closing my eyes, I hit the gas,
knowing I'd be a pillar of salt
if I looked back.

The Feathered Thing

Emily Dickinson called Hope
a feathered thing, like a bird that flies.
I'd call it something that floats.

Perhaps a helium balloon.
Imagine brightly colored balls
drifting upward to the clouds
on a warm summer day.

How do I describe the necessity of Hope?
How its absence is rocks, weighing down
the pockets of a gypsy girl
in a Yiddish story I read years ago.

She stepped into the river
long hair flowing behind her,
until every strand disappeared.

Maybe she was right.
There is no cosmic vending machine.
No button for dispensing the beverage I desire.

But I still reach
with both arms, fingers wiggling,
for the feathered thing
to pull me from the water
and lift me to the sky
where I can float,
however briefly,
as a brightly colored ball.

Facing the Wilderness

Twelve scouts went into Canaan.
Ten saw giants too big to fight
while two saw grapes too big to carry.

"We are like grasshoppers in the land,"
the ten cried, "sure to be crushed."
"Not true," Joshua and Caleb argued.

Steadfast, they predicted victory
while the rest shrieked and mourned
imagined defeat. In the end,
only the two survived
to stand on promised land.

An instructive tale for me
as I consider the faith needed
to see grapes instead of giants
in the wilderness waiting ahead.

Even When I Turn Away

Shimmering ripples
paint a staircase
on the water,
leading my eyes
to the source of light

until I look away,
wincing.

I can't explain
the fury of foamy waves
knocking down a loved one
dragging him by the ankles

on the same beach
where sandpipers sprint—
twig legs chasing
every morsel spotted.

Speckled wings
soar over sparkling questions
round as the orb in the sky.

Even when I turn away, I feel
a presence on my skin.

Cactus

Right now, my life
resembles a desert plant
with spines too sharp
to embrace.

Still, giant green limbs
raised like towers
against blue sky
tempt me to look up.

So do bright flowers
bearing fruit
over barren ground.

And I'm intrigued
by those succulent stems,
staunchly protecting
internal moisture
no matter how seldom
rain appears.

Handling Knives

To sauté onions, you must
peel and dice amid tears.
Apples don't bake in a pie
with stems and seeds.
Even a bagel needs a blade
to separate halves and schmear.

If we want to cook,
we must handle knives,
expose tender flesh
to razor sharp edges.
Nothing worth tasting
escapes the risk of blood.

Waiting To Heal

Fractured bone
bleeds, then clots.
A callus forms
and tissue toughens—
as long as
circulation is good,
no infection intrudes,
and the limb
stays immobile
long enough.

Bone cells
possess the magic
to link broken parts,
become whole enough
to bear the weight
of living once again.

If only waiting
weeks and weeks
didn't blister and itch
or entomb every thought
inside a plaster crypt.

The Consolation of Clouds

In its gaseous state,
water is colorless and odorless,
so imperceptible,
it could be called imaginary.
But when this same
colorless vapor condenses
miles above the ground
majestic white mountains
appear in a blue diamond sky.

And the sunlight,
streaming through
serrated shapes
feels like fingers
reaching down
to wipe the tears
from my cheeks.

To Be A Gold Droplet Floating

While sometimes
prayer dissolves me
like sugar in water
to become
a sweeter substance,
I am just as satisfied
with suspension
in this oil and vinegar world—
to be a gold droplet floating
in a dark, mysterious sea
certain
I can withstand
a hard shaking
and not be absorbed
by bitter circumstances.

Mourner's Prayer

Help me,
squeeze the joy
from each moment
like toothpaste from a tube.

To press a little harder
and seek whatever still remains
to freshen the taste on my tongue.

ACKNOWLEDGEMENTS: The author would like to thank the following publications where the listed poems in *Itzhak Perlman's Broken String* first appeared:

"Avocado Secret" *Bourgeon*
"Cactus" *Germ Magazine*
"The Consolation of Clouds" *YARN Magazine*
"Even When I Turn Away" *NoVA Bards Anthology*
"Itzhak Perlman's Broken String" *Apeiron Review*
"Facing the Wilderness" *Jewish Women's Literary Annual*
"The Feathered Thing" *Dirty Chai*
"A Game Played With Helmets" *Empty Sink Publishing*
"Handling Knives" *Postcards Poems and Prose Magazine*
"Ladies Lunch" *Apeiron Review*
"Letter to 30 Year Old Self" *The Lake*
"Mitzi's Obit" *Empty Sink Publishing*
"Preparing for Disaster" *Folia Literary Magazine*
"Punctuated Text" *The Lake*
"Re-Watching the Titanic" *Germ Magazine*
"Squatter" *Steam Ticket*
"To Be a Gold Drop Floating," winner *Spirit First Contest*
"Two Dirt Roads" *Lowestoft Chronicle*
"Train Therapy" *Aji Magazine*
"Two Elderly Aunts" *All Roads Will Lead You Home*
"Waiting to Heal" *Blood and Thunder*
"The Village Not Reached" *Apeiron Review*